© 2003 Algrove Publishing Limited
ALL RIGHTS RESERVED.
No part of this book may be reproduced in any form, including photocopying, without permission in writing from the publishers, except by a reviewer who may quote brief passages in a magazine or newspaper or on radio or television.

Algrove Publishing Limited
36 Mill Street
Almonte, Ontario K0A 1A0

Telephone: (613) 256-0350
Fax: (613) 256-0360

National Library of Canada Cataloguing in Publication Data

Mr. Punch with rod and gun : the humour of fishing and shooting : with 193 illustrations / by Charles Keene ... [et al.].

(Classic reprint series)
ISBN 1-894572-73-4

1. Fishing--Humor. 2. Hunting--Humor. 3. Fishing--Caricatures and cartoons.
4. Hunting--Caricatures and cartoons. 5. English wit and humor. 6. English wit and humor, Pictorial. I. Keene, Charles, 1823-1891 II. Series: Classic reprint series (Almonte, Ont.)

PN6231.F5M56 2003   799'.02'07   C2003-901446-0

Printed in Canada
#10703

Publisher's Note

The Humour of Fishing and Shooting is one of the 25 volumes in the 1925 Punch Library of Humour. An original volume was made available to us from the library of Bryn Matthews of Almonte, Ontario, Canada.

Leonard G. Lee, Publisher
Almonte, Ontario
July 2003

PUNCH LIBRARY OF HUMOUR
Edited by J. A. HAMMERTON
◢ Designed to provide in a series
of volumes, each complete in itself,
the cream of our national humour,
contributed by the masters of
comic draughtsmanship and the
leading wits of the age to "Punch,"
from its beginning in 1841 to the
present day ◢   ◢   ◢   ◢

MR. PUNCH WITH ROD
AND GUN

A FEAT OF AGILITY.—*Voice from the Bow (to Binks, who is trying to adjust the moorings, and has arrived at the happy moment when he is doubtful whether he will stay with the pole or return to the punt).* " Now then, you idiot, keep still! I've got a nibble!"

MR. PUNCH
WITH ROD AND GUN

THE HUMOURS OF FISHING
AND SHOOTING

WITH 193 ILLUSTRATIONS

BY

CHARLES KEENE, JOHN LEECH,
PHIL MAY, GEORGE DU MAURIER,
L. RAVEN-HILL, C. SHEPPERSON,
CECIL ALDIN, BERNARD PART-
RIDGE, W. J. HODGSON, A. S.
BOYD, TOM BROWNE, REGINALD
CLEAVER, CHARLES PEARS, H. M.
BROCK, AND OTHERS

PUBLISHED BY SPECIAL ARRANGEMENT WITH
THE PROPRIETORS OF "PUNCH"

𝕕 𝕕 𝕕

THE EDUCATIONAL BOOK CO. LTD.

THE PUNCH LIBRARY OF HUMOUR

Twenty-five volumes, crown 8vo, 192 pages
fully illustrated

PREFACE

As a fisherman MR. PUNCH is in the best of his humours. He makes merry over the weaknesses of those who follow the craft of Old Izaak, always with the slyest of genial manners. The angler's habit of exaggerating the size of his catch—his patience or his impatience when the fish won't bite—the conscious or unconscious ridicule he has to endure from onlookers when he is unsuccessful—the proverbial thirst that attacks the fisherman, whether he catches anything or not—MR. PUNCH has a keen eye for all such incidentals

and presents them so jovially that nobody laughs over them more heartily than his victims themselves do.

Leech, Charles Keene, Phil May, Du Maurier, Raven-Hill, Bernard Partridge, G D. Armour—most of the best-known PUNCH artists, old and new, have revelled in the humours of both fishing and shooting.

He gets as much laughter out of those who handle the gun. The infinite variety of jokes he cracks about the bad shot, the man who can't hit the birds, or is always hitting the dogs or his companion guns, is amazing. He does not spare the lady shooter, and jests of the peril in which the rest of the field are placed when she is out after the birds or rabbits; and he gets a good deal of fun out of the Frenchman's alien notion of sport.

" POTTING SHRIMPS "

MR. PUNCH WITH ROD
AND GUN

Observations on Ground Bait.—Boys are often taught, though they never learn, to regard fishing as a cruel amusement, when nevertheless angling, at least as most commonly practised in the Thames, is universally admitted to be particularly and pre-eminently the *gentle* craft.

Epitaph on an Angler.—" Hooked it.

THE DUFFER WITH A SALMON-ROD

FROM "THE CONFESSIONS OF A DUFFER"

No pursuit is more sedentary, if one may talk of a sedentary pursuit, and none more to my taste, than trout-fishing as practised in the South of England. Given fine weather, and a good novel, nothing can be more soothing than to sit on a convenient stump, under a willow, and watch the placid kine standing in the water, while the brook murmurs on, and perhaps the kingfisher flits to and fro. Here you sit and fleet the time carelessly, till a trout rises. Then, indeed, duty demands that you shall crawl in the manner of the serpent till you come within reach of him, and cast a fly, which usually makes him postpone his dinner-hour. But he will come on again, there is no need for you to change your position, and you can always fill your basket easily—with irises and marsh-marigolds.

Such are our country contents, but woe befall the

" What bait are yer usin', Billie ? "   " Cheese."
" What are yer tryin' ter catch—mice ? "

9

"A SALMON TAKING A FLY"

day when I took to salmon-fishing. The outfit is expensive, "half-crown flees" soon mount up, especially if you never go out without losing your fly-book. If you buy a light rod, say of fourteen feet, the chances are that it will not cover the water, and a longer rod requires in the fisherman the strength of a Sandow. You need wading-breeches, which come up nearly to the neck, and weigh a couple of stone. The question has been raised, can one swim in them, in case of an accident? For *one*, I can answer, he can't. The reel is about the size of a butter-keg, the line measures hundreds of yards, and the place where you fish for salmon is usually at the utter ends of the earth. Some enthusiasts begin in February. Covered with furs, they sit in the stern of a boat, and are pulled in a funereal manner up and down Loch Tay, while the rods fish for themselves. The angler's only business is to pick them up if a

TRIALS OF A NOVICE.—*Friend (in the distance).* "Enjoying it, old chap?"   *Novice.* "*Rather!*"

II

salmon bites, and when this has gone on for a few days, with no bite, influenza, or a hard frost with curling, would be rather a relief. This kind of thing is not really angling, and a Duffer is as good at it as an expert.

Real difficulties and sufferings begin when you reach the Cruach-na-spiel-bo, which sounds like Gaelic, and will serve us as a name for the river. It is, of course, extremely probable that you pay a large rent for the right to gaze at a series of red and raging floods, or at a pale and attenuated trickle of water, murmuring peevishly through a drought. But suppose, for the sake of argument, that the water is "in order," and only running with deep brown swirls at some thirty miles an hour. Suppose also, a large presumption, that the Duffer does not leave any indispensable part of his equipment at home. He arrives at the stream, and as he detests a gillie, whose contempt for the Duffer breeds familiarity, he puts up his rod, selects a casting line, knots on the kind of fly which is locally recommended, and steps into the water. Oh, how cold it is! I begin casting at the top of the stream, and step from a big boulder into a hole.

Diminutive Nursemaid (to angler, who has not had a bite for hours). "Oh, please, sir, do let baby see you catch a fish!"

13

Stagger, stumble, violent bob forwards, recovery, trip up, and here one is in a sitting position in the bed of the stream. However, the high india-rubber breeks have kept the water out, except about a pailful, which gradually illustrates the equilibrium of fluids in the soles of one's stockings. However, I am on my feet again, and walking more gingerly, though to the spectator my movements suggest partial intoxication. That is because the bed of the stream is full of boulders, which one cannot see, owing to the darkness of the water. There was a fish rose near the opposite side. My heart is in my mouth. I wade in as far as I can, and make a tremendous swipe with the rod. A frantic tug behind, crash, there goes the top of the rod! I am caught up in the root of a pine-tree, high up on the bank at my back. No use in the language of imprecation. I waddle out, climb the bank, extricate the fly, get out a spare top, and to work again, more cautiously. Something wrong, the hook has caught in my coat, between my shoulders. I must get the coat off somehow, not

"Not Proven."—*Presbyterian Minister.* "Don't you know it's wicked to catch fish on the Sawbath?!" *Small Boy (not having had a rise all the morning).* "Wha's catchin' fesh?!"

15

Old Gent. (*who has recently purchased the property*). " Now, don't you boys know that nobody can catch fish in this stream except with my—er—a—special permit ? "
   Youthful Angler. " Get away ! Why, me and this 'ere kid's catched scores of 'em wi' a worrum ! "

an easy thing to do, on account of my india-rubber armour. It is off at last. I cut the hook out with a knife, making a big hole in the coat, and cast again. That was over him ! I let the fly float

Angler (after landing his tenth—reading notice). "The man who wrote that sign couldn't have been using the right bait!"

down, working it scientifically. No response.
Perhaps better look at the fly. Just my luck, I
have cracked it off!

Where is the fly-book? Where indeed? A
feverish search for the fly-book follows—no use : it
is not in the basket, it is not in my pocket ; must
have fallen out when I fell into the river. No good
in looking for it, the water is too thick, I *thought*
I heard a splash. Luckily there are some flies in
my cap, it looks knowing to have some flies in one's
cap, and it is not so easy to lose a cap without
noticing it, as to lose most things. Here is a big
Silver Doctor that may do as the water is thick. I
put one on, and begin again casting over where that
fish rose. By George, there he came at me,
at least I think it must have been at me, a great
dark swirl, " the purple wave bowed over it like a
hill," but he never touched me. Give him five
minutes law, the hook is sure to be well fastened
on, need not bother looking at that again. Five
minutes take a long time in passing, when you are
giving a salmon a rest. Good times and bad times
and all times pass, so here goes. It is correct to
begin a good way above him and come down to

MISPLACED SYMPATHY.—"Well? Have you caught any fish, Billy?" "Well, I *really* caught *two*! But they were quite young, poor little things, and so they *didn't know how to hold on!*"

him. I'm past him ; no, there is a long heavy drag
under water, I get the point up, he is off like a shot,
while I stand in a rather stupid attitude, holding on.
If I cannot get out and run down the bank, he has
me at his mercy. I do stagger out, somehow,
falling on my back, but keeping the point up with
my right hand. No bones broken, but surely he is
gone ! I begin reeling up the line, with a heavy
heart, and try to lift it out of the water. It won't
come, he is here still, he has only doubled back.
Hooray ! Nothing so nice as being all alone when
you hook a salmon. No gillie to scream out con-
tradictory orders. He is taking it very easy, but
suddenly he moves out a few yards, and begins
jiggering, that is, giving a series of short heavy
tugs. They say he is never well hooked, when he
jiggers. The rod thrills unpleasantly in my hands,
I wish he wouldn't do that. It is very disagreeable
and makes me very nervous. Hullo ! he is off
again up-stream, the reel ringing like mad : he gets
into the thin water at the top, and jumps high in
the air. He is a monster. Hullo ! what's that
splash ? The reel has fallen off, it was always
loose, and has got into the water. How am I to

TRIALS OF A NOVICE

Angler. " Hush! Keep *back!* Keep *back!* I had a
beautiful rise just then; shall get another directly."

21

act now ? He is coming back like mad, and all the line is loose, and I can't reel up. I begin pulling at the line to bring up the reel, but the reel only lets the line out, and now he's off again, down stream this time, and I after him, and the line running out at both ends at once, and now my legs get entangled in it, it is twisted all round me. He runs again and jumps, the line comes back in my face, all slack, something has given. It is the hook, it was not knotted on firmly to start with. He flings himself out of the water once more to be sure that he is free, and I sit down and gnaw the reel. Had ever anybody such bad fortune? But it is just my luck !

I go back to the place where the reel fell in, and by pulling cautiously I extract it from the stream. It shan't come off again ; I tie it on with the leather lace of one of my brogues. Then I reel up the slack, and put on another fly, out of my cap— a Popham. Then I fish down the rest of the pool. Near the edge, in the slower part of the water, there is a long slow draw ; before I can lift the point of the rod, a salmon jumps high out of the water at me,—and is gone ! I never struck him,

DREADFUL SITUATION!

Party in Waders (on the shallower side, with nice trout on).
" Now then, you idiot, bring me the net, can't you, or he'll
be off in a second!"

was too much taken aback at the moment; did not expect him then. Thank goodness, the hook is not off this time.

The next stream is very deep, strong and narrow; the best chance is close in on my side. By Jove! here he is, he took almost beside the rock. He sails leisurely out into the strength of the stream; if he will come up, I can manage him, but if he goes down, the water is very swift and broken, there are big boulders, and then a sheer wall of rock difficult to pass in cold blood, and then the Big Pool. He insists on going down; I hold hard on him, and refuse line. But he leaps, and then— well he *will* have it; down he rushes, I after him, over the stones, scrambling along the rocky face; great heavens! *the top joint of the rod is loose;* I did not tie it on, thought it would hold well enough. But down it runs, right down the line; it must be touching the fish. It is; he does not like it, he jiggers like a mad thing, rushes across the Big Pool, nearly on to the opposite bank. Why won't the line run? The line is entangled in my boot-lace. He is careering about; I feel that I am trembling like a leaf. There, I knew it would

"Deuced odd, Donald, I can't get a fish over seven pounds, when they say Major Grant above us killed half a dozen last week that turned twenty pounds apiece!" *Donald.* "Aweel, sir, it's no that muckle odds i'th' sawmon,—but thae fowk up the watter is bigger leears than we are doon here!"

25

happen; he is off with my last casting-line, hook and all. A beauty he was, clear as silver and fresh from the sea. Well, there is nothing for it but a walk back to the house. I have lost one fly-book, two hooks, a couple of casting-lines, three salmon, a top joint, and I have torn a great hole in my coat. On changing my dress before lunch, I find my fly-book in my breast pocket, where I had not thought of looking for it somehow. Then the rain comes, and there is not another fishing day in my fortnight. Still, it decidedly was "one crowded hour of glorious life," while it lasted. The other men caught four or five salmon apiece; it is their red letter day. It is marked in black in my calendar.

To Well-Informed Piscatorials.—*Query*. What sort of fish is a Nod?

Note. A Nod is a sea-fish, and is, probably, of the limpet tribe. This we gather from our knowledge of the Periwinkle, known in polite circles as the 'Wink. The value of the Nod has come down to us in the form of an old proverb, "A Nod is as good as a 'Wink," and this no doubt originated the query to which we have satisfactorily replied.

"ONE GOOD TURN," ETC.—*City Man (to one of his clerks he finds fishing in his ornamental water).* "Look here, Smithers, I've no objection to giving you a day now and then 'to attend your aunt's funeral'.—but I think you might send some of the fish up to the house!"

MISSED.—*Angus.* "Eh, man, that wass a splendid cod! If we had gotten that cod, noo, we micht ha' been ha'ein' a dram." *Mr. Smith (from Glasgow).* "Indeed, and ye would, Angus." *Bauldry.* "Mebbe, Maister Smuth, if we wad have had a dram afore ye wass lettin' doon yer line, we micht have grappit that muckle fush!"

Friend. "Hullo, old chappie! Fallen in?"

Dripping Angler. "You don t suppose this is a perspiration, do you?"

29

THE GENTLE CRAFTSMAN (?).—*Irascible Angler (who hasn't had a rise all day).* "There!"—(*Throwing his fly-book into the stream, with a malediction*)—"Take your choice!"

30

UNLUCKY.—*American Cousin (last day of season).* " What sport ? 'Guess I've been foolin' around all day with a twenty-five-dollar pole, slinging fourteen-cent baits at the end of it, and haven't caught a darned fish ! "

"THERE'S MANY A SLIP," ETC.—Waggles saw a splendid three-pound trout feeding in a quiet place on the Thames one evening last week. Down he comes the next night, making sure of him! But some other people had seen him too!!

Contemplative Man in punt). "I don't so much care about the sport, it's the delicious repose I enjoy so."

MENACE

Little Angler (to her refractory bait). "Keep still, you tiresome little thing! If you don't leave off skriggling, I'll throw you away, and take another!"

A BLANK DAY

Old Gent (greeting friend). "Hullo, Jorkins! 'Been
fishing? What did you catch?"
Jorkins (gloomily). "Ha'-past six train home!"

C 2

AN OBVIOUSLY UNKIND INQUIRY

Brown (to Jones, who has, for the first time, been trying his hand at fishing from a boat). "Well, old chap, what sort o' sport?"

SEIZING HIS OPPORTUNITY

The Major (on his way to try for the big trout, and pondering on his fly-book). "Now I wonder what he'll take? What d'you say, Smithers, eh?" *Smithers (pulling up with alacrity).* "Take, sir? Well, sir, thanky, sir, sup o' whisky, sir, for choice!"

37

CONSCIENTIOUS FLATTERY.—*Boatman.* "I canna mind a finer fesh for its size!"

WET AND DRY.—*Careful Wife.* " Are you very wet, dear ? " *Ardent Angler (turning up his flask).* " No; dry as a lime-kiln—haven't had a drop these two hours!"

DRY-FLY ENTOMOLOGY. — (Scene — *The banks of a Hampshire stream in the grayling season*). *Angler (the rise having abruptly ceased).* "I think they're taking a siesta, Thompson." *Keeper.* "I dessay they are, sir, but any other fly with a touch o' red in it would do as well."

40

EGOMANIA.—(Scene—The Bar Parlour of the "Little Peddlington Arms," during a shower.) Little Peddlingtonian (handing newspaper to stranger from London). "Have you seen that account of our fishing competition in the Little Peddlington Gazette, sir?" "No, I'm afraid I've not!" 'It's a very interesting article, sir. It mentions my name several times!"

BOTTOM FISHING.—*Piscator No.* 1 (*miserably*). "Now, Tom, *do* leave off. It isn't of any use, and it's getting quite dark." *Piscator No.* 2. "Leave off!! What a precious disagreeable chap you are! You come out for a day's pleasure, and you're already wanting to go home!"

TRIALS OF A NOVICE.—*Unfeeling Passer-by.* "Say, mister! Are you fly-fishing, or 'eaving the lead?"

Piscator, Senior. "What! yer want to chuck it up jus because we never catches nothing. Why, I'd like to know how yer proposes to spend the remainder of yer 'olidays, eh?"

A BROAD HINT

Piscator. "Yes, I like a day at this time of year. Get all the *water to myself*, you see."

Yokel. "Ah! And mayhap have a sup o' the whisky to spare for somebody else, governor?"

Tom (writing).—"I say, Bob, I'm rubbing in the local colour for the benefit of the folk at home—could you help me to some correct *fishing* expressions—just to give the thing an atmosphere?"

Bob. "I've heard a lot one time and another, old man, but the only one I remember is—'*Pass the flask*'!"

46

"MIGHT BE WORSE!"—*First Folly Angler (peckish after their walk).* "Got the sandwiches and——" *Second Folly Angler (diving into creel).* "Oh, yes, here they are, all right, and here's the whisk—but—tut-t-t, by Jove!—I've forgotten the fishing-tackle!!" *First Folly Angler.* "Oh, ne' mind—we'll get along quite well without *that!*"

REBUS IN ARDUIS

TELL me, stranger, ere I perish,
　Of the fish men call the trout,
Fre I lose the hopes I cherish,
　Summer in and summer out,
Hopes of hooking one and landing
　Him before the day is done,
Waist deep in the water standing,
　From the dawn to set of sun.

Tell me, *is* his belly yellow?
　Is he spotted red and black?
Does he look a splendid fellow
　When you turn him on his back?
Is there any fly can rise him,
　Any hook can hold him tight?
Is one able to surprise him
　Any time from morn to night?

Stranger, years I've passed in trying
　Every artifice and lure,
Standing, crawling, wading, lying,
　Casting clean and long and sure.
Empty yet remains my basket,
　Cramped and weary grows my fist,
Stranger, in despair I ask it,
　Does the trout in truth exist?

HAGIOLOGY.—*Patron of a Fishmarket.*—St. Poly-
carp.

ENCOURAGING PROSPECT.—*Piscator Juvenis.* " Any sport, sir ? " *Piscator Senex.* " Oh, yes ; very good sport." *P. J.* " Bream ? " *P. S.* " No ! " *P. J.* " Perch ? " *P. S.* " No ! " *P. J.* " What sport, then ? " *P. S.* " Why, keeping clear of the weeds ! "

TEACHING THE TEACHER.—*New Curate.* "Now, boy, if, in defiance of that notice, *I* were to bathe here, what do you suppose would happen?" *Boy.* "You'd come out a great lot dirtier than you went in!"

"SMALL MERCIES."—*First Jolly Angler (with empty creel).*
"Well, we've had a very pleasant day! What a delightful
pursuit it is!"   *Second Ditto (with ditto).*   "Glorious!
I sha'n't forget that nibble we had just after lunch, as long
as I live!"   *Both*   "Ah!!"

"VERY LIKELY A WHALE"

Lady Visitor (who has been listening to Piscator's story). " I didn't know that trout grew as large as that ! "

Piscator's Wife. " Oh, yes, they do—after the story has been told a few times ! "

A REFLECTION BY AN ANGLER.—Nature's aristocracy. Mortal man being but a worm, is therefore by nature of *gentle* birth.

———

NET PROFIT.—A fisherman's.

———

PISCATORIAL.—Shakespearian angler's song to his bait : " Sleep, gentle, sleep."

Our Friend Briggs contemplates a Day's Fishing.—He is here supposed to be getting his tackle in order, and trying the management of his running line.

53

Robson. "Do you think fishes can hear?"
Dobson. "I should *hope* not. Listen to old Smith—he's smashed his rod!"

54

Lambertson (who is nervous, and weighs about a cart-load of bricks, to Dapperton, who has just nipped across, and weighs about nine stone nothing). " Oh, yes ! All very fine for you to say, ' Don't dwell on it,' b—b— BUT——"

THE GENTLE CRAFT

(*By Our Own Trout*)

How gentle is the fisherman who sits beside the brook,
And firmly puts the wriggling worm upon the pointed hook
How pleasant for the hapless trout to find, from some
strange cause,
The fly conceals a something that makes havoc with its
jaws!

Dame Juliana Berners wrote a book, in which she said
The blessing of St. Peter rests upon the angler's head;
She bid him not be " ravenous in taking game,"—I wish
She'd ever asked if he deserved the blessings of the fish.

We were a happy family, as merry as could be,
" Diversified with crimson stains," as Pope has said. Ah me!
There came the cruel fisherman, his flies had deadly gleam,
And not a soul remains but me to mourn within the stream.

What recked my little troutlets of the Palmers, Spinners,
Duns,
They headlong rushed, and then got caught, my innocent
young sons!
They're cooked—excuse an old trout's tear!—but hard it is
to feel
A monster's ta'en your family for matutinal meal:

The " honest angler," Walton, cried, and maundered night
and day,
But Byron puts the matter in a very different way;
He said that Isaac should have hook fixed firmly " in his
gullet,"
And oh! that I might be the trout that he suggests should
pull it.

Brown (enthusiastic angler, who has brought his friend and guest out for a "delightful day's fishing"). "Confound it! I've left them—I say, old chap, got any flies with you?" *Jones (not enthusiastic, and a non-smoker, wearily).* "Flies!!!"

CATS WHO CATCH CAN

Uncle George, just returned from a morning's fishing, recounts how he landed some of the " most magnificent trout ever taken in these waters," and his audience antici- pate much satisfaction from the contents of his basket.

Meanwhile the contents of Uncle George's basket are being fully appreciated in the hall !

Lunatic (*suddenly popping his head over wall*). " What **are you**
doing there ? " *Brown.* " Fishing." *Lunatic.* " Caught anything ? " *Brown.* " No." *Lunatic.* " How long have you been
there ? " *Brown.* " Six hours." *Lunatic.* "*Come inside !*"

A GENTLE HINT.—*Mr. Giglamps (who has been caught by keeper with some fish in his basket under taking size).* "Oh—er—well, you see, fact is, my glasses—er—magnify a good deal. Make things look larger than they really are!" *Keeper (about to receive smaller tip than meets the occasion).* "Ah! makes yer put down a shillin' when yer means 'alf-a-crown, sometimes, I dessay, sir!"

PAYING TOO DEAR FOR HIS WHISTLE.—*Donald*. "E—h, sir, yon's a gran' fesh ye've gotten a haud o'!" *The Laird*. "Oo, aye, a gran' fesh enoo, but I'd be gay an' glad if I saw my twa-and-saxpenny flee weel oot o' his mooth!"

Jones (the adventurous). " It—it's gettin' almost too d-deep, I fear, Miss Hookem ! "

Miss Hookem. " Oh, please do go on ! It'll be the fish of my life ! "

Jones (who is not a champion swimmer). " M-mine too ! "

AN ACUTE ANGLER.—The judicious Hooker.

ANGLER'S MOTTO.—*Carpe diem.* A carp a day.

THE ANGLE OF INCIDENCE.—When you're fishing, and tumble into the water.

WALTON'S LIFE OF HOOKER.—Is this another name for Izaak Walton's *Complete Angler ?*

HINTS TO BEGINNERS—SEA FISHING

In fishing for conger eels, it is sometimes convenient
to have a spare boat.

RETURNED EMPTY.—*Old Mayfly (who had dropped his flask further down stream, and has just had it returned to him by honest rustic).* "Dear me! Thank you! Thank you!" (*Gives him a shilling.*) "Don't know what I should ha' done without it!" (*Begins to unscrew top.*) "May I offer you a——" *Honest Rustic.* "Well, thank y', sir, but me and my mate, not seein' a howner about, we've ta'en what there were inside."

HINTS TO BEGINNERS.—When casting with a fly rod, be sure to get
your line well out behind you.

THE COMPLEAT DUFFER

Hooking a lobster

I HAVE fished in every way,
Fished on every kind of day,
But my basket still remains *in
statu quo*,
Not a stickleback will rise,
Not a gudgeon as a prize
To the quite amazing flies
That I throw.

When I try the purling brook
Many trout just have a look
At my fly, or at the minnow that I spin,
With fishy leer they squirm
Off, and my belief is firm
That I'd better use a worm
On a pin.

Wherever I get leave,
Still I fish from morn to eve,
Though I never—hardly ever—rightly cast,
With a body soaking wet,
With a mind intent and set
On success achieving yet
At the last.

In my coat of wondrous tweed,
And on every wandering weed,
Hooks and flies unnamed invariably I fix.
Here I cannot land a fish—
I can only hope and wish
I may creel a goodly dish
In the Styx.

66

RELIEF.—*Piscator (about the end of a very bad day).* "Donald, hang the boat here a bit, we may get a rise." *Donald.* "Hang!"—*(Giving way)*—"I shall tamm the boat if you will, and the trouts—and the loch too!"

[*Feels better!*

67

E 2

Catching her-ring

Deep C fishing

Q. What is the difference between a dunce and an angler?

A. One hates his books and the other baits his hooks.

———

ENTHUSIASTIC. — That indefatigable angler, Trollinson, never forgets his craft. Even in writing to you, he is sure to drop a line.

Catching min'nose on
the bridge

First instance of the cure of
soles (*Vide* Life of St. Anthony)

SUPERB

Podgson (a recently joined disciple of the gentle craft). " Ah, now I flatter myself that I played that fellow with considerable skill, and landed him without the net, too ! "

" I'll punch your 'ead, directly, if you don't leave orff.
How do yer think the what's-a-names 'll bite, if you keep
on a splashin' like that ? "

AN ORIGINAL CORNER MAN.—*The Complete
Angler.*

———

A BROTHER OF THE ANGLE. — A fellow
mathematician.

———

WHEN is a fisherman like a Hindoo ? When
he loses his cast.

Irate Landowner (to Angler). "Hi, you, sir! This is *my* water.
You can't fish here." *Angler.* "Oh, all right. Whose is that
water up there round the bend?" *Irate Landowner.* "Don't know:
not mine. But this is." *Angler.* "Very well. I'll wait till that
flows down here!"

'MANY A SLIP.'—*Boisterous Friend (bursting suddenly through the shrubbery, and prodding proprietor with his umbrella).* "Hul-lo, Hackles, my boy! Ketching lots o' salmon!" *Angler.* "There! Tut-t-t—confound you! I should ha' settled that fish if you hadn't come bothering about! Three people coming to dinner without notice, and only chops in the house! You'd better go and tell my wife what you've done

PISCATORIAL POLITENESS. (*From a Yorkshire stream.*)—*Privileged Old Keeper* (*to member of fishing club, of profuse and ruddy locks, who is just about to try for the big trout, a very wary fish*). "Keep yer head doon, sir, keep yer head doon!" (*Becoming exasperated.*) "'Ord bou it, man, keep yer head doon! Yer m't as weel come wi' a torch-leet procession to tak' a fish!"

SOMETHING LIKE PRESERVATION.—*Irate Individual.* " Are you aware, sir, that you are fishing in preserved water? " '*Arry (not quite so innocent as he would appear).* " Preserved water ! And is all the fish *pickled*, then ? Bless'd if I've seen any live 'uns about."

Mrs. Brown. "Well, I must be going in a minute."

Mr. B. "What for?"

Mrs. B. "Why, I forgot to order the fish for dinner."

More Ornamental than Useful.—"Just give that bit o' lead a bite atween yer teeth, will yer, matie?" "Ain't ye got no teeth of yer own?" "I got some, but there ain't none of 'em opposite one another."

ANTICIPATION.—Piscator (*short-sighted; he had been trolling all day for a big pike that lay in a hole about here*). "Quick, Jarvis—the landing-net—I've got him!" *Jarvis.* "Ah, sir, it's only an old fryin'-pan! But that will be useful, y'know, sir, when we do catch him!"

A PUNT POEM

I'M a fisherman bold,
And I don't mind the cold,
Nor care about getting wet through;
I don't mind the rain,
Or rheumatical pain,
Or even the tic-douloureux!

I'm a fisherman damp,
Though I suffer from cramp,
Let weather be foul or be fine,
From morning till night
Will I wait for a bite,
And never see cause to repine!

I'm a fisherman glad,
And I never am sad;
I care not to shoot or to hunt;
I would be quite content
If my whole life were spent
From morning to night in a punt!

I'm a fisherman brave,
And I carol a stave
In praise of the rod and the line!
From the bank, or a boat,
Will I gaze on my float—
What life is so happy as mine?

Big Scotchman. "Confound these midges!"
Little Cockney. "Why, they 'aven't touched me!"
Big Scotchman. "Maybe they have na noticed ye yet!"

THE GREATEST ANGLE OF ELEVATION.—
Fishing off the top of Shakespeare's Cliff.

BAIT AND WHITEBAIT

THE " gentle " craft some people angling name;
The "lobworm" might more truly call the same.

First Angler (to country boy). "I say, my lad just go to my friend on the bridge there, and say I should be much obliged to him if he'd send me some bait."

Country Boy (to second angler, in the Eastern Counties language). "Tha' there bo' sahy he want a wurrum!!"

THE LAY OF A SUCCESSFUL ANGLER

THE dainty artificial fly
  Designed to catch the wily trout,
Full loud *laudabunt alii*,
  And I will join, at times, no doubt,
But yet my praise, without pretence,
Is not from great experience.

I talk as well as anyone
  About the different kinds of tackle,
I praise the Gnat, the Olive Dun,
  Discuss the worth of wings and hackle
I've flies myself of each design,
No book is better filled than mine.

But when I reach the river's side
  Alone, for none of these I wish,
No victim to a foolish pride,
  My object is to capture fish;
Let me confess, then, since you ask it—
A worm it is which fills my basket!

O brown, unlovely, wriggling worm,
  On which with scorn the haughty look,
It is thy fascinating squirm
  Which brings the fattest trout to book,
From thee unable to refrain,
Though flies are cast for him in vain!

Catching crabs and flounders
in the Thames

Catching wails at
Whippingham

Deep gratitude to thee I feel,
    And then, perhaps, it's chiefly keen,
When rival anglers view my creel,
    And straightway turn a jealous green;
And, should they ask me—" What's your fly ? "
" A fancy pattern," I reply !

Catching soles and skate on the
(sea) Serpentine

Catching whiting from
the Strand

SOMETHING LIKE A CATCH.—*Mrs. Binks* (*sick of it*).
"Really, John! How can you bear to spend your time
whip—whip—whipping at the stream all day long and
never a single fish taking the least notice of you?"
John. "Ah, but think o' the delight, Maria, when you do
get a fish! Lor' bless us, my dear, have you forgotten the
day when you hooked me?"

FROM DEE-SIDE.—*Piscator.* "Yes, my boy, ain't he a beauty? Forty pounds—three foot eight from tail to snout—fresh run! I'm going to have him photographed, with a full-grown man standing by, to show the proportions. By the way"—*(faintly)*—"would—er—would *you* mind being the *man ?*"

Imperturbable Boatman. "Hand up yer rod, man! Ye have 'm! ye have 'm!"

ANECDOTE BY IZAAK WALTON.—One Piscator, whom I will not further name, had a certain acquaintance who, through the credit he had gotten by his wealth, worth, and wit, came to be made a magistrate. Whereupon Piscator goes me to the river and catches a fish, which having brought home, he sends to the new-made justice with a note, saying, "Inasmuch, sir, as you are now promoted to the condition of a beak, I do send you a perch."

ANGLING EXTRAORDINARY

Customer (in a great hurry). " A small box of gentles, please.
And look sharp !   I want to catch a 'bus ! ! "

A SPORTIVE SONG

*A Sojourner in North Britain goes Salmon-fishing
with a New Young Woman.*

FAR from the busy haunts of men,
  'Mid hazel, heather, gorse,
You are the Beauty of the glen,
  And I the Beast, of course.
I fetch and carry at your wish,
  I wait your beck and nod,
And yet your soul is with that fish,
  Your ardour in your rod.

He struggles hard, gives now a lunge,
  Like boxer in the ring,
And now he executes a plunge
  That makes your tackle spring;
And then again he quiet lies,
  As if in cunning thought
Of how to lose this worst of flies
  That he so gladly caught.

Anon we see his silver back
  Rush madly up the stream,
And then he takes another tack,
  An effort that's supreme;
He tries to leap the rocky wall
  That environs the pool.
How hot that rush! How low that fall!
  While you are calm and cool.

88

Visitor. " Are there any fish in this river ? "
Native. " Fish ! I should rather think there was. Why, the
water's simply saturated with 'em ! "

You utter not a word; your wrist
  Must surely be of steel;
For, let your captive turn or twist,
  You never spend the reel.
But with your eye fast fixed you stand—
  Diana with a hook—
Determined that good grilse to land,
  And bring your fly to book.

Well done! He weakens! With the gaff
  I'm ready for the prey.
And now you give a little laugh
  That means " He must give way ! "
" Look out ! " you cry. I do look out,
  And then I lose my head.
You've missed the fish without a doubt,
  But captured me instead !

A POINT OF TRESPASS.—*Irate Owner of this side of water.* "Are you aware that you are trespassing in this water, young man ? "

Sharp Youth. "But I'm not in the water, sir."

Irate Owner (more irate). "Confound you, but you've just taken a fish out ! "

Sharp Youth. "Yes, sir. The fish was trespassing ! "

Enthusiastic Fisherman. "What a bore ! Just like my luck. No sooner have I got my tackle ready, and settled down to a book, than there comes a confounded bite ! "

Angling in the Serpentine.—Saturday, p.m.—*Piscator No. 1.* "Had ever a bite, Jim?
Piscator No. 2. "Not yet—I only come here last Wednesday!"

A Bad Bargain.—No water!—and after having rented a stream, and travelled five hundred miles, too !!

Di would go sea-fishing to-day. I went too. She says we had a grand day, so I suppose we had. At the same time, I don't think it was quite right to give my lunch to the boatman without asking me whether I wanted it or no. Di says she'll ask her cousin—hang him!—to go with her next time.

Irate Angler waking tramp). "Why can't you look after your beast of a dog? It's been and eaten all my lunch."

Tramp (hungrily). "What, all the lot, mister! Well, he shouldn't ave done that if *I* could 'ave 'elped it!"

94

SHAKSPEARIAN MOTTO FOR AUGUST 12

" Now will I hence to seek my lovely moor! "
Titus Andronicus, Act II., Sc. 3.

THE BIRDS AND THE PHEASANT

(*After Longfellow*)

I SHOT a partridge in the air,
It fell in turnips, " Don " knew where;
For just as it dropped, with my right
I stopped another in its flight.

I killed a pheasant in the copse,
It fell amongst the fir-tree tops;
For though a pheasant's flight is strong,
A cock, hard hit, cannot fly long.

Soon, soon afterwards, in a pie,
I found the birds in jelly lie;
And the pheasant, at a fortnight's end,
I found again in the *carte* of a friend.

95

ODE ON A DISTANT PARTRIDGE

(By an Absent-minded Sportsman)

WELL, I'm blest! I'm pretty nearly
    Speechless, as I watch that bird,
Saving that I mutter merely
    One concise, emphatic word—
    What that is may be inferred!

English prose is, to my sorrow,
    Insufficient for the task.
Would that I could freely borrow
    Expletives from Welsh or Basque—
    One or two is all I ask!

Failing that, let so-called verses
    Serve to mitigate my grief
Doggerel now and then disperses
    Agonies that need relief.
    (Missing birds of these is chief!)

Blankly tramping o'er the stubbles
    Is a bore, to put it mild;
But, in short, to crown my troubles,
    One mishap has made me riled,
    Driv'n me, like the coveys, wild.

For at last I flush a partridge,
    Ten yards rise, an easy pot!
Click! Why, bless me, where's the cartridge?
    Hang it! there, I clean forgot
    Putting *them* in ere I shot!

"TURN ABOUT."—*George.* "I say, Tom, do take care! You nearly shot my father then!" *Tom.* "'Sh! Don't say anything, there's a good fellow! Take a shot at mine!!"

THE FOOL WITH A GUN

(To the Tune of the " Temptation of St. Anthony ")

A LITTLE CHECK

THERE are many fools that worry
    this world,
  Fools old, and fools who're young;
Fools with fortunes, and fools
    without,
Fools who dogmatise, fools who
    doubt,
Fools who snigger, and fools who
    shout,
Fools who never know what they're
    about,
  And fools all cheek and tongue;
Fools who're gentlemen, fools
    who're cads,
Fools who're greybeards, and fools
  who're lads;
Fools with manias, fools with fads,
Fools with cameras, fools with tracts,
Fools who deny the stubbornest facts,
Fools in theories, fools in acts;
  Fools who write Theosophist books,
  Fools who believe in Mahatmas and spooks;
Fools who prophesy—races and Tophets—
Bigger fools who believe in prophets;
Fools who quarrel, and fools who quack;
In fact, there are all sorts of fools in the pack,
  Fools fat, thin, short, and tall;
But of all sorts of fools, the fool with a gun
(Who points it at someone—of course, "in fun"—
And fools around till chance murder is done)
  Is the worstest fool of them all!

HIS FIRST PARTRIDGE SHOOT

SPORTING EXTRAORDINARY—THE OLD DOG POINTS CAPITALLY

"I tell yer wot it is, Sam! If this fool of a dog is a going to stand still like this here in every field he comes to, we may as well shut up shop, for we shan't find no partridges!"

TRIALS OF A NOVICE.—"Confess now. Have you ever hit a haystack, even?"
"What did you aim at?"   "Well, of course I have."

THE FIRST OF SEPTEMBER

THE First of September, remember
    The day of supremest delight.
Get ready the cartridge, the partridge
    Must fall in the stubble ere night.

The breechloader's ready, and steady
    The dog that we taught in old days;
He's firm to his duty, a beauty
    That cares for but one person's praise.

He's careful in stubble, no trouble
    In turnips, he's keen as a man;
But looks on acutely, and mutely
    Seems saying, " Shoot well, if you can ! "

They flash from the cover—what lover
    Of sport does not thrill as they rise
In feathered apparel ?   Each barrel
    Kills one, as the swift covey flies.

So on through the morning, still scorning
    All rest until midday has past,
When lunch should be present, and pleasant
    That *al fresco* breaking of fast.

One pipe, then be doing, pursuing
    The sport that no sport can eclipse ;
So homeward to dinner, a winner
    Of praise from the fairest of lips.

A HUMANE INSTINCT.—*Snob (who has been making himself very objectionable).* "I say, what do you do with your game?" *Host.* "Give my friends what they want, and send the rest to market." *Snob.* "Ah, sell it, do you? With my game, don'tyer-know , I give my friends some, and send the rest to the hospitals." *Host.* "And very natural and proper, I'm sure. The only thing I've seen you shoot to-day was a beater ! "

Husband. " Look out, Kitty. There are some birds just in front of you ! "
Wife (out for the first time). " Then, for goodness sake, keeper, call that silly dog of yours ! Can't you see he's standing right in my way ? "

AN UNFORTUNATE REMARK.—Novice (to host, after walking for two hours under a brilliant sun without seeing a single bird). "Grand day, isn't it?" [N.B.—He only meant to lighten the general depression, but he wasn't invited again.

A WISE PRECAUTION

Sportsman (to his wife, who is rather a wild shot.) "By Jove! Nelly, you nearly got us again, that time! If you are not more careful, I'll go home!"

Old Keeper (sotto voce). "It's all right, squire. Her bag is full of nothing but *blank* 'uns!"

"GUNNING WITH A SMELL DOG"

(B. Jonathan, Esq., having missed a hare, the dog drops to the shot)

B. J. (scornfully). " Call that a good dawg ? I reckon he ain't worth candy ! When the beast's sitting, he stands and looks at him ; and when he runs away, he lies down and looks at me ! "

Keeper. " Would you gentlemen kindly tell me which of you two is a lord, *as I've been told to give him the best place.*"

Gentleman. " That looks a well-bred dog."

Owner. " I should think he was well-bred. Why, he won't have a bit er dinner till he's got his collar on ! "

SS. PATRICK AND PARTRIDGE

" Now at the birds, me boy, let dhrive ! "
Says Mike, exhorting Dan.
" That's how we'll keep the game alive,
By killing all we can ! "

DAMAGED GOODS.—*Sportsman (invited to help shoot some bucks in Mr. Meanman's park, and has just knocked one over).* "By Jove! what a lovely head! You must let me have that for mounting." *Mr. Meanman (frightfully indignant).* "What! cut his head off! Why, man, it would ruin the sale of the carcase!"

UNNECESSARY QUESTIONS.

Lady (*with gun*). "Am I holding the thing right?"

Sportsman (*to Snobson, who hasn't brought down a single bird all day*). " Do you know Lord Peckham ? " *Snobson.* " Oh dear, yes ; I've often shot at his house." *Sportsman.* " Ever hit it ? "

III

Renting a well-stocked moor   A shooting party

A ZOOLOGICAL CONUNDRUM. — *Intending Tenant* (*to* Lord Battusnatch's *Head Keeper*). And how about the birds? Are they plentiful, Gaskins?

Gaskins. Well, sir, if the foxes of our two neighbours was able to lay pheasants' eggs, I should say there'd be no better shooting south o' the Trent.

SAD FATALITY TO ONE OF A SHOOTING PARTY ON THE MOORS.—On returning home, after a most successful day's sport, just as he entered the garden he was taken from life by a snap-shot.

A Blank Day.—*First Friend.* " The birds are terribly
wild to-day."

Second Friend. " Not half so wild as our host will be, if
it keeps on like this."

At a Dog-Show.—*First Fancier.* That's a
well-bred terrier of yours, Bill.

Second Fancier. And so he ought to be. Didn't
the Princess of Wales own his great grand-aunt!

Choke bore

Birds were strong

THE ANATOMY OF SHOOTING

MEN WE NEVER MEET

1. The man who makes no excuses for shooting badly; such as—1. The light was in his eyes; 2. He was bilious; 3. There was something wrong with his cartridges; 4. Too many cigars the night before; 5. Some particular eatable or drinkable taken the night before; 6. Or that morning; 7. He was afraid of hitting that beater; 8. We were walking too fast; 9. He hadn't got his eye in; 10. Or his eye was out; 11. He didn't think it was his bird; 12. It was too far off; 13. He always thought there was something the matter with *that* gun.

2. The man whose dog hasn't a good nose.

3. The man who can't "shoot a bit sometimes."

4. The man who hasn't some particular theory as to—1. The very best gun; 2. Cartridges;

THE FIRST OF SEPTEMBER. (*Our sporting French friend, voted dangerous, has been given a beat to himself.*)—*Chorus.* " Well, Count, what luck ? "   *Count.* . " Magnifique ! I have only shot one ! Mais voilà ! Qu'il est beau ! The King partridge ! Regardez ses plumes ! N est ce pas ? "

Marking black game

Small bags—one brace

3. Charges of powder and shot; 4. Best tipple to shoot on; 5. Best sort of boots; 6. Gaiters; 7. And equipment generally.

5. The man who doesn't change the said theory every season.

6. The man who hasn't sometimes said he couldn't shoot after lunch.

7. Or that he could shoot better after lunch.

8. The man who on your remarking that your friend George Lake is a good shot, doesn't answer that you should see Billy Mountain (or someone else) and then you would know what shooting really was.

9. The man who hasn't a friend who " can't hit a haystack."

10. The friend who owns it.

11. The man who doesn't like to be considered a good shot.

"EVERY EXCUSE."—*Brigson (excited).* "Hullo!—There goes a——" (*Ups with his gun!*) *His Host (clutching his arm).* "Good Heavens!—You're not going to shoot that fox?" *Brigson.* My dear filer! wh'-wh'-why not? This is the last day I shall have this season—and I—I feel as if I could shoot my own mother-in-law—if she rose!"

Giving 'em both barrels

Dropped his bird

12. The man who, being a bad shot, doesn't comfort himself by thinking he knows a worse.

13. The man who hasn't made a longer shot than anyone in the company.

14. The man who, having made it, doesn't tell the story.

15. And who, having told the story, doesn't tell it more than once.

Finally, *Mr. Punch* is never likely to meet the man who, having read the above, will not own that it is strictly true of those who pursue the pleasant pastime of shooting when, as the eminent Burton puts it, "they have leisure from public cares and business."

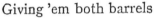

SONG OF "THE MISSING SPORTSMAN"

How happy could I be on heather,
A-shooting at grouse all the day,
If only the birds in high feather
Would not, when I shoot, fly away!

Brown (after an hour's digging for the ferret). "Call this rabbit shootin'? I call it landscape gardening!"

"So you don't think much of my retrievers ? "
"On the contrary.   I think you have two most valuable watch dogs."

"ONCE HIT TWICE SHY."—*Guest* (*taking keeper aside*).   "Look here, Smithers" — (*gives half-a-sov.*)—"Put me out o' gunshot of the Squire. He does shoot so precious. wild, and my nerve isn't what it used to be!"

"Ground Game."—*Wife.* "Ah, then you've been successful at last, dear!" *Husband (prevaricating).* "Ye—yes, I bagged——" *Wife (sniffing).* "And *high* time you did! I should say by the— oh!—it must be cooked to-day!"

[*It came out afterwards the impostor had bagged it at the poulterer's*

SCENE—*A shooting party, August 12 (M. F. H. is introduced to distinguished foreigner)*

"You hunt much of the fox, monsieur? I also, and have already of him shot twenty-five, and have wounded many more!"

His "First".—*Brown (good chap, but never fired a gun in his life).* "I say, you fellows, I don't mind confessing that I am a bit nervous, you know. I hope none of you will pepper me!"

LE SPORT

[The French sportswoman is not ardent, but just now
Le Sport is the thing."—*Daily Paper*.]

Ze leetle bairds zat fly ze air
　　I vish zem not ze 'arms—
Zat is not vy ze gun I bear
　　So *bravement* in mine arms ;
'Tis not zat I vould kill—*Ah ! non !*
　　It is zat I adore
Ze noble *institution*
　　Ve call in France *Le Sport.*

And zen ze costume !　Ah !　ze 'at !
　　Ze gaitares !　Vot more sweet
For ze young female-chaser zat
　　Do 'ave ze leetle feet ?
Ze gun ?—I fear 'im much, and oh !
　　'E makes my shouldare sore,
But yet I do 'im bear to show
　　'Ow much I love *Le Sport.*

Ze leetle partridge 'e may lay
　　'Is pretty leetle eggs,
Ze leetle pheasant 'op away
　　Upon 'is leetle legs,
Ze leetle 'are zat run *si vite*
　　I do not vish 'is gore—
But vile mine ankles zey are neat
　　I'll cry, " *Ah !　Vive le Sport !* "

124

Keeper (to beater). "What are you doin' here? Why don't ye go and spread yourself out?"
Beater. "Zo I were spread out, and t'other man 'e told I, I were too wide!"

Master Bob. "I say, Adam, that was a pretty bad miss"

Keeper. "'Twasn't even that, Master Bob. 'Twas firing in a totally wrong direction."

"Beg pardon, sir! But if you was to aim *at* his lordship the next time, I think he'd feel more comforbler, sir!"

LOVE AMONG THE PARTRIDGES

SEPTEMBER's first, the day was fair,
  We sought the pleasant stubble,
The birds were rising everywhere,
  The old dog gave no trouble.
And still my friend missed every shot,
  While I ne'er fired in vain.
I said, "Perchance the day's too hot?"
  He cried, "Amelia Jane!"

We shot throughout the livelong day,
  We always shoot together,
And yet in a disgraceful way,
  He never touched a feather.
I said, "How is it that you muff
  Your birds, my boy? Explain."
He sighed and said, "I know it's rough
  But, oh, Amelia Jane!"

Quoth I, "Amelia Jane may be
  As plump as any partridge,
But that's no reason I can see
  Why you should waste each cartridge."
He shot the dog, then missed my head,
  But caused the keeper pain;
Then broke his gun and wildly fled
  To join Amelia Jane!

"ENOUGH OF IT."—*Country Squire.* "By George! Tom, you've gone and shot the dog!" *Friend (from town).* "O, I say, old fellow, let's go back and have a game o' billiards, or else I'm quite sure I shall shoot the other one! They keep getting in the way so!"

HINTS TO BEGINNERS.—Lion hunting.   Be quite sure when you go looking for a lion, that you really want to find one.

THE POET GOETH GUNNING

"Hare up!"

Hot work

THE GROUSE THAT JACK SHOT

(*A Solemn Tragedy of the Shooting Season*)

THIS is the Grouse that *Jack* shot.

This the friend who expected the Grouse that *Jack* shot.

This is the label addressed to the friend who expected the Grouse that *Jack* shot.

This is the Babel where lost was the label addressed to the friend, &c.

This is the porter who " found " the " birds " in the Babel where lost was the label, &c.

This is the dame with the crumpled hat, wife of the porter who " found " the " birds," &c.

This is the cooking-wench florid and fat of the dame with the crumpled hat, &c.

This is the table where diners sat, served by the cooking-maid florid and fat of the dame with the crumpled hat, &c.

This is the *gourmand* all forlorn, who dreamed of the table where diners sat, served by the cooking-wench florid and fat, &c.

This is the postman who knocked in the morn awaking the *gourmand* all forlorn from his dream of the table, &c.

And this is *Jack* (with a face of scorn), thinking in wrath of " directions " torn from the parcel by railway borne, announced by the postman who knocked in the morn, awaking the *gourmand* all forlorn, who dreamed of the table where diners sat, served by the cooking-wench florid and fat of the dame with the crumpled hat, wife

A BLANK DAY.—"Well, dear, did you get anything?" "Not a thing! I only fired once, and that was more out of spite than anything else!"

of the porter who "found" the "birds" in the Babel
where lost was the label addressed to the friend who
expected the Grouse that *Jack* shot !

MORAL.

If in the Shooting Season you some brace of birds would
send
(As per letter duly posted) to a fond expectant friend,
Pray remember that a railway is the genuine modern Babel,
And be very very careful *how you fasten on the label !*

"WEDDED TO THE MOOR"

THE sportive M.P., when the Session *is* done,
Is off like a shot, with his eye on a gun.
He's like *Mr. Toots* in the Session's hard press,
Finding rest "of no consequence."   Could he take less ?
But when all the long windy shindy is o'er,
He, like *Oliver Twist*, is found "asking for *Moor !*"

A HINT IN SEASON

REMEMBER, remember,
The month of September—
Partridges, rabbits, and hares ;
Any hamper you send,
My breech-loading friend,
Put "Paid" on the label it bears.

SPORTIANA.—A young sportswoman in the
Highlands is reported to have shot "six fine stags
through the heart."   Must have been "young
bucks."   Of course, she used Cupid's bullets on
her murderous career amid the harts.

"A MOST PALPABLE!"

Beginner (*excitedly, the first shot at the end of a blank morning*). " How's that, John ? "

John. " Well, ye seem to 'ave 'it 'im, sir ! "

ON A DANGEROUS SHOT

(By Mr. Punch's Vagrant)

HE seemed an inoffensive man
   When first I saw him on the stubble ;
Made on the self-same sporting plan
   As those who shoot with ease or trouble !
The average men, in fact, whose skill
   (A thing of luck far more than habit)
Tempts them at times to go and kill
   The hare, the partridge and the rabbit.

He rushed not and he did not lag ;
   He kept the line when we were walking.
He had a useful cartridge-bag ;
   And was not prone to useless talking.
He smoked an ordinary pipe ;
   His guns were hammerless ejectors ;
He wore a fairly common type
   Of patent pig-skin leg-protectors.

He told a story now and then,
   Some ancient tale of fur or feather,
That sportsmen love to smile at when
   On Autumn days they come together.
In fact, he seemed to outward view
   In all his gunned and gaitered glory,
Just such a man as I or you,
   Except—but that's another story.

THE SINEWS OF SPORT.—*The Marquis (to head keeper).* " Now, Grandison, His Royal Highness will be tired of waiting ; why don't you send in the beaters ? " *Head keeper (sotto voce).* " Beg pardon, my lord, the London train's late this morning with the pheasants—we must have half an hour to get 'em into the coverts ! "

Except (I'll tell it) when he shot:
   Then, then he did not care a cuss, sir ;
He blazed as if he hadn't got
   The least regard for life or us, sir.
Our terrors left him unafraid ;
    He tried for full-grown birds and cheepers,
And, missing these, he all but made
   A record bag of guns and keepers.

AT THE QUICKSHOT CLUB.—*First Sportsman.*
Well, I killed four rabbits with two barrels last
September.

Second Sportsman. And I had five partridges
on one drive, three coming towards me, and two
with fresh cartridges over the hill.

Third Sportsman (wearily). But nobody comes
up to my slaying of an elephant in Assam with a
pea rifle. Would you like to hear the yarn ?

[*The Third Sportsman is immediately left*
                   alone.

MR. PUNCH has pleasure in directing the atten-
tion of sportsmen of his own limited stature to an
advertisement in the *Field* announcing the sale of
an estate, " including fifty acres of sporting woods,
together with a small gentleman's residence."

138

HIS FIRST BIRD

"Well, I didn't miss *that* one, at all events!" "No, sir. They *will* fly into it, sometimes!"

Circumstances over which he has no control oblige the Pater to celebrate the *glorious twelfth* in town this year. With the help of the poulterer, and the boys (at home for the holidays), he enjoys such excellent sport, that he says " never no moor" will he lavish hundreds of pounds on what he can get for next to nothing at home.

ONE WAY OF LOOKING AT IT!—*Delinquent (to his host).* " Oh, I'm most unfortunate! Now, you're the third man I've hit to-day!"

Sportsman (*who has just shot a duck*). "I think he'll come down, Duncan."

Duncan. "Ay, sir, he'll come down—when he's hungry."

"THE GLORIOUS FIRST"

Young Newstyle (justly indignant, to Squire Oldacres).
"There!—'Knew how it would be when you *would* bring
out those beastly dogs. *Always in the way, hang 'em!*"

BROTHERLY CANDOUR.—*Jack* (*to lady, come out to lunch*). "Are you coming with the guns this afternoon, Miss Maud?" *Miss Maud.* "I would, but I don't think I should like to see a lot of poor birds shot!" *Jack.* "Oh, if you go with Fred, your feelings will be entirely spared!"

A RISKY PROCEEDING.—*Mr. Pipler (of Pipler & Co.) is having his first day on his recently-acquired moor. Any amount of shooting. Bag, absolutely—nothing.* Master Pipler (after much thought). "Of course, they are far too valuable to be killed and eaten, pa. But isn't it rather dangerous to frighten them so much? I heard ma saying they cost you at least a guinea a brace!"

TRIALS OF A NOVICE

Old Hand. " Now, for the last time, for goodness' sake
don't shoot any of us, or the dogs, or yourself."

Novice (sarcastically). " What about the birds ? "

Old Hand. " Oh, you won't hit them ! "

MR. MUGGS' GROUSE MOOR

Mr. Muggs leaves for the north. Mr. M. as he appeared, half a minute before the train started, minus half of his luggage, and with the guard shouting to him to take his seat!

"Pheasant-shooting in some districts will suffer through lack of birds. The wet weather has been fatal to the young broods."—*Shooting Reports*.

Head Keeper (on the First). "Werry sorry, my lord, but this 'ere's th' on'y one as we've manisht to rare. Will I put it up for your lordship?"

148

Beater to hare that refuses to leave her form). "Get oop, ye lazy little beggar an' join in t' spoort!"

SHOOTING PROSPECTS

Johnnie Bangs. "I say, old man, do you mind taking these cartridges out? I've never used a gun before, don't you know!"

THE END OF THE SEASON.—*Passing Friend.* "Hulloa, Jack! Why on earth are you hiding there?" *Jack.* " Only safe place, don't you know. Governor's giving the tenants a day to finish the covers. They've just about finished two dogs and a beater already!"

THE "CHEEP" OF THE PART-RIDGE

Perdix Cinerea loquitur

'Tis the voice of the sportsman. I hear him complain,
"All my hopes of big bags have been damped by the rain.
With birds shy and scarce, flooded furze and no stubble,
To beat dripping covers is scarce worth the trouble."
Aha! The wind's ill that blows nobody good,
True, the wet has proved fatal to many a brood,
Parent birds have made moan over eggs swamped and
    addled,
When our covers were lakes in which ducks might have
    paddled,
But partridges drowned when they'd scarce chipped the
    shell,
Yet,—yes, on the whole, 'tis perhaps just as well.
Water! Better than fire ; and a cold in the head
Is not *quite* so bad as a dose of cold lead.
Prime time for swell vassals of powder and shot !
What's September to them, without plenty to pot ?
Oh! won't they fume, as they look out this morn
On these damp furzy swamps, and yon drenched standing
    corn ?
Poor grumbling gun-maniacs ! Isn't it fun ?
In the game " Birds *v.* Barrels " we birds will score one
Just for once, I should hope. In this beautiful bog
I am safe, I should fancy, from man, gun, and dog.

HINTS TO BEGINNERS. GROUSE DRIVING

Birds coming straight towards you sometimes offer a very unsatisfactory shot.

153

They may bag a few birds on the skirts of the wheat,
But I don't think *this* cover will pay 'em to beat.
St. Partridge be bothered! St. Swithin's *my* Saint,
May his rainy rain last, *I* shall make no complaint.
No! Farmers and sportsmen may grumble together—
For my part, I rather approve of the weather.

[*Left chuckling.*

OVER THE STUBBLE.—*Mr. Winchester Poppit
(at the luncheon by the coppice).* I must say that I
like to see partridges driven.

*Captain Treadfoot Trotter (who believes in shoot-
ing over dogs).* No doubt, Mr. Poppit, you'd like
to see the poor birds driven in a coach, or a tandem,
or a curricle; or, if I may judge by the way you
sent my pointer round the last field, ye'd wish to
put 'em in a circus!

WILD SPORTS.—*The Sportsmen (from the
wood).* "Hullo, Tonsonby! You've had a good
place. We've heard you blazing away all the
afternoon. How many have you bagged?"

Tonsonby (a town man). "O, bother your tame
pheasants. I've tree'd a magnificent tom cat here,
and had splendid sport, but I can't hit him. You
come and try!"

RATHER STARTLING

"Well, Count! Any sport this morning?"

"Hélas! mon ami, very sad sport! I'ave shot three beautiful misses!"

[*He means he has missed three beautiful shots.*

HER "FIRST"

Miss Nimrod. "Oh, dear! he's pointing! Which end do I shoot at?"

Out after partridges. Unluckily, tripped up just as Di's cousin got in the way. Thought Di rather unnecessarily sympathetic, as he was by no means dangerously hit.

RISKY

Mr. O'Fluke (whose shooting has been a bit wild). " Very odd, Robins, that I don't hit anything ? "

Robins (dodging muzzle). " Ah, but a'm afeard it's ower good luck to continue, sir ! "

MR. TUBBING'S SHOOTING PONY

159

RATHER PROUD OF IT.—*Landlord (who is having a shoot for his tenant-farmers).* "Good Heavens, Mr. Mangold! That bird can't have been more than a couple of feet over Mr. Butter's head!" *Mr. Mangold.* "Oh! That's what I call *shootin'!*"

MISTAKEN VOCATION.—*Major Missemall (an enthusiast on sporting dogs).* "Confound the brute! That's the dog I was going to run in the retriever trials, too. But I won't now. I'd reserve him for the Waterloo Cup."

Friend. "I wouldn't. I'd

DERISION.—*Bagnidge (to his friend's keeper).* "Tut-t-t-t—dear me! Woodruff, I'm afraid I've shot that 'og!" *Keeper.* "Oh no, sir, I think he's all right, sir. He mostly drop down like that if anybody misses!!"

ECHO ANSWERS.—*Short-sighted swell (to gamekeeper, who has been told off to see that he "makes a bag")* "Another hit, Wiggins! By the way—rum thing—always seem to hear a shot somewhere *behind* me, just after I fire!" *Wiggins (stolidly).* "Yes, sir, 'zactly so, sir. Wunnerfle place for echoes this 'ere, sir!"

BALLAD OF THE CUNNING PARTRIDGE

THE partridge is a cunning bird,
  He likes not those who bring him down :
From age to age he has preferred
  The shots that blaze into the brown,
Whose stocks come never shoulder high,
  Who never pause to pick and choose,
But on whose biceps you descry
  The black, the blue, the tell-tale bruise.

Or should a stubborn cartridge swell,
  And jam, as it may chance, your gun,
The sly old partridge knows it well,
  " Great Scott ! " he seems to chirp " here's fun ! "
He gathers all his feathered tribe,
  They leave the stubble or the grass,
And with one wild and whirling gibe
  Above your silent muzzles pass.

Your scheme you carefully contrive,
  And, while each beater waves his flag,
Your fancy, as they duly drive,
  Already sees a record bag.
But lo ! they baulk your keen desire,
  For, though with birds the sky grows black,
Not one of them will face the fire,
  And every blessed bird goes back.

HINTS TO BEGINNERS.—When going out before daylight after ducks, waders are advisable. Also, better tell your wife she need not come down (just when you expect the ducks) and ask if you are sure you are not getting your feet wet.

165

A NOVELTY

Mr. Cylinder (who always uses his host's cartridges). " What powder are these loaded with, my boy ? "

Beater. " Ar doan't rightly know ; but ar think they calls it serdlitz pooder ! "

For partridges I'll try no more ;
　Why should I waste in grim despair ?
Take me to far Albania's shore,
　And let me bag the woodcock there.
Or on the Susquehanna's stream
　I'll shoot with every chance of luck
The gourmet's glory and his dream,
　The canvas-back, that juicy duck.

*Disgusted Keeper (who has just beaten up a brace or 30 of pheasants,
which young Snookson has missed " clane and clever "—to dog, which
has been " going seek " and " going find " from force of habit).* " Ah,
Ruby, Ruby, bad dog! T' heel, Ruby, t' heel! Ah must apologise
for Ruby, sir. You see, Ruby's been accustomed to pick 'em up ! "

Mr Punch with Rod and Gun

Yea, any other bird I'll shoot,
    But not again with toil and pain
I'll tramp the stubble or the root,
    Nor wait behind a fence in vain.
For of all birds you hit or miss
    (I've tried it out by every test),
Again I say with emphasis
    The partridge is the cunningest.

An extended tract of moor

A second laying

Heavy bags are difficult to
secure

168

Extract from a private letter. "Our bag on the first was *barely* up to the average, although the mater, Milly, and self were out to help the men. We hunted in couples and threes, as it is a bit dull tramping along alone. And as the mater generally foozles her shots, I did most of her work too. By the way, how absurdly nervous men are 'gunning.'"

MR. MUGGS ON PARTRIDGE DRIVING

"What I like about the modern system of driving is the nice rest you can have between the beats."

LITTLE CHICKMOUSE RASHLY ACCEPTS THE OFFER OF A DAY'S PARTRIDGE-SHOOTING.—*Game-keeper (to Little C., who has kicked up a hare).* "Now for it, sir!" *Chickmouse (who finds he can't get over his horror of firearms).* "Well—fact is—I'd rather you'd —— Look 'ere, you 'old the gun, and I'll pull the thingummy!!"

"A HIT! A PALPABLE HIT!"

"Oh, I beg your pardon! I did not see you, sir!"
"See me! Confound it, sir, you can see *through* me,
now!"

THE STATE OF THE GAME.—*Lady Customer.* "How much are grouse to-day, Mr. Jiblets?" *Poulterer.* "Twelve shillings a brace, ma'am. Shall I send them——" *Lady Customer.* "No, you need not send them. My husband's out grouse-shooting, and he'll call for them as he comes home!"

EDUCATED. (*From a Yorkshire moor*).—*Keeper* (*to the Captain, who has missed again, and is letting off steam in consequence*). "Oh dear! Oh dear! It's hawful to see yer missin' of 'em, sir; but"—(*with admiration*)—"ye're a scholard i' langwidge, sir!"

SELF-CONFIDENCE OUT SHOOTING.—*Nephew.* "Jump, uncle! I'll clear you!"
[*But he didn't "clear" him, and old Brown says he'll carry the marks to his grave!*

"I don't know what it is. Mark, but I can't hit a bird to-day!"

"Let's see your gun, sir. Ah!—well, I'd try what you could do *with some cartridges in it*, if I was you, sir!"

BREAKING IT GENTLY.—*Son of the House (who wishes to say some-thing polite about our friend's astounding shooting, but who cannot palter with the truth).* "I should think you were awfully clever at books, sir!"

A TRUE SPORTSMAN

(*A last shot of the season*)

Old Pothunter. "Always show mercy, my boy, always show mercy! Much better to shoot 'em sitting, and save poor things a nasty fall!" [*Does.*

TRIALS OF A NOVICE

Brown. "I wish I had the moral courage to go home!"

M 2

SPORT!—*Cockney Sportsman (eager, but disappointed).* "I say, my boy, seen any birds this way?" *'Cute Rustic (likewise anxious to make a bag).* "Oh, a rare lot, guv'nor—a rare lot—just flew over this 'ere 'edge, and settled in that 'ere field, close to Squire Blank's ricks." [*Cockney sportsman tips boy a shilling, and goes hopefully after . . . a flock of starlings!*

His Lordship (after missing his tenth rabbit). " I'll tell you what it is, Bagster.   Your rabbits are *all two inches too short,* hereabouts ! "

PLEASANT FOR HARRY

Fair Sportswoman. "Oh, Harry, I feel so excited, I scarcely know what I am doing!"

BLANK FIRING

Ancient Sportsman (whose sight is not what it used to be).
" Pick 'em up, James, pick 'em up! Why don't you pick
'em up ? "

Veteran Keeper. " 'Cause there bean't any down, my
lord ! "

SPORT IN SPORT

(Game played by Dumb-Crambo, Junior)

Cartridges

Stubble and turn-up

Marking down

A breech loader

Hairs and part-ridges
were scarce

Full cock

Boy (after watching old sportsman miss a couple of rocketers). "Have you shot often, uncle?" *Uncle.* "Yes, my boy, a great deal. At one time, in Africa, I used to live by my gun." *Boy (thoughtfully).* 'Did you? And is that why you're so thin?"

Fitz. "I say, are *all* your beaters out of the wood?" *Keeper.* "Yes, sir." *Fitz.* "Are you sure?" *Keeper.* "Yes, sir." *Fitz.* "Have you *counted* them?" *Keeper.* "No, sir; but I know they're a right." *Fitz.* "Then I've shot a roe deer!"

"LE SPORT."—*Keeper.* "Why didn't you fire the other barrel, m'seer—the other barrel at the last bird?" *Monsieur Alphonse.* "Bah! I did fire ze odher barrel! I do fire bodt barrels togezzer! And in my own country I do shoot ze lark at twenty, twenty-five, and sometimes dirty yards—when he stand quite still! Your dogs zey make ze birds to fly away",—*(insinuatingly)*—"and zey must be fatigued. Here is money. Take zem, and buy zem somezings to eat! Leave me to make my own dogs myself!!"

BEHIND THE SCENES.—*Beater.* "'Ere you are, Mr. Bags, 'ere's another one, but 'e bain't too fresh. I don't think 'e were killed to-day." *Keeper (sotto voce).* "'Old your row, stupid ! Of course he wasn't. We always puts a few down where the gov'nor's goin' to stand !"

The Laird (to little Tomkins, who is being initiated into the mysteries of deer-stalking). "Don't move a step
Lie down where you are!"

HOW MOSSOO SHOT THE COCK-PHEASANT

(*The Gamekeeper's Story*)

HE were a sort o' Frenchman, sir,
  And called hisself a Duck:
I never could make head or tail
  O' that there furrin muck!

He came to stay wi' Master there.
  And brought his guns and that—
But bless you, sir! he could na' shoot,
  No more than this here hat!

The Master and the Frenchman went
  To shoot the spinney-kivver
What reaches from the stable-wall
  Right down to that there river.
A rocketing cock flew up at wunst,
  And Mossoo he fired, and missed—
How he did swear, and tear his hair,
  And shake his little fist!

Mr. Punch with Rod and Gun

The way that Mossoo danced about,
  It really were a sight!
He'd grin, and pull his beard, and shout
  And screech with all his might.
He wore a thing across his nose
  Just like a kind o' shear:
I think he said he were " my hop "—
  Which means his sight were near.

Mossoo he yelled, "I see him zere,
  Upon ze stable top!"
With that he banged off right and left—
  I seed a summat drop;
I ran to pick up that there bird;
  And 'neath the stable-clock
I found it sure enow—it were
  Our new gilt weather-cock!

BRADBURY, AGNEW, & CO. LTD., PRINTERS, LONDON AND TONBRIDGE.